Uruguay

Everything You Need to Know

Introduction to Uruguay

Nestled in the southeastern region of South America lies a captivating land of rich history, vibrant culture, and stunning natural beauty - Uruguay. Despite its small size, Uruguay boasts a diverse landscape, stretching from the rolling plains of the interior to the picturesque coastline along the Atlantic Ocean. As one of the continent's smallest countries, Uruguay is often overshadowed by its larger neighbors, Argentina and Brazil, but its unique charm and character make it a hidden gem waiting to be explored.

With a population of just over 3 million people, Uruguay is known for its warm and welcoming atmosphere. The country's capital and largest city, Montevideo, is a bustling metropolis that serves as the cultural, economic, and political center of Uruguay. Here, visitors can immerse themselves in the vibrant street life, explore historic neighborhoods, and indulge in the city's thriving culinary scene.

Beyond the urban hustle and bustle, Uruguay's countryside beckons with its tranquil beauty and rural charm. The interior of the country is dominated by vast expanses of fertile farmland, where traditional estancias (ranches) dot the landscape. Here, visitors can experience the timeless allure of gaucho culture, with its roots in the country's rich agricultural heritage.

Uruguay's coastline is another highlight, with miles of pristine beaches, charming seaside towns, and rugged cliffs offering breathtaking views of the Atlantic Ocean. From the glamorous resort town of Punta del Este to the quaint fishing village of Cabo Polonio, there's something for everyone along Uruguay's picturesque coast.

But perhaps the true essence of Uruguay lies in its people. Known for their warmth, friendliness, and laid-back attitude, Uruguayans take pride in their country's progressive values and strong sense of community. From lively street festivals to intimate family gatherings, the spirit of camaraderie is palpable throughout Uruguay.

As we embark on our journey to discover everything there is to know about Uruguay, let us delve deeper into the country's rich history, explore its diverse culture, savor its delectable cuisine, and uncover the hidden treasures that make Uruguay a truly special place to visit.

Geography and Climate: Exploring Uruguay's Diverse Landscape

Uruguay's geography is as diverse as it is captivating, offering a blend of landscapes that range from rolling plains to sandy beaches and lush forests. Situated in the southeastern part of South America, Uruguay shares borders with Argentina to the west and Brazil to the north, with the vast Atlantic Ocean bordering its eastern coastline.

The country's terrain is predominantly flat, with the fertile plains of the interior known as the pampas dominating much of the landscape. Here, vast stretches of grassland provide ideal conditions for agriculture, making Uruguay one of the world's leading producers of beef and wool.

In contrast to the flat interior, Uruguay's coastline offers a striking contrast, with sandy beaches, rocky cliffs, and pristine bays stretching for over 400 miles along the Atlantic Ocean. From the bustling resort town of Punta del Este to the remote beauty of Cabo Polonio, the coast is a playground for sun-seekers, surfers, and nature enthusiasts alike.

Further inland, the landscape gives way to rolling hills and river valleys, where picturesque vineyards and olive groves thrive in the temperate climate. The Uruguay River, which forms part of the border with Argentina, meanders through the western part of the country, providing vital water resources for agriculture and transportation.

Despite its relatively small size, Uruguay boasts a remarkable variety of ecosystems, including wetlands, forests, and marshes, which are home to a rich diversity of plant and animal life. The Bañados del Este Biosphere Reserve, located near the city of Rocha, is a prime example of Uruguay's commitment to conservation, protecting vital habitats for migratory birds and other wildlife.

In terms of climate, Uruguay experiences a temperate maritime climate, characterized by mild winters and warm summers. The moderating influence of the Atlantic Ocean helps to keep temperatures relatively stable throughout the year, with average highs ranging from the 50s°F (10s°C) in winter to the 80s°F (20s°C) in summer.

Rainfall is evenly distributed throughout the year, although the southern regions tend to receive slightly more precipitation than the north. This balanced climate provides favorable conditions for agriculture, with fertile soils and ample sunshine supporting a wide range of crops, including soybeans, corn, and citrus fruits.

Overall, Uruguay's diverse geography and climate make it a unique and inviting destination for travelers seeking to explore the natural beauty and cultural heritage of this fascinating country. From the rolling plains of the interior to the pristine beaches of the coast, there's something for everyone to discover in Uruguay's diverse landscape.

Early Settlement and Indigenous Heritage

The early settlement of Uruguay dates back thousands of years, with evidence of human habitation found throughout the region. Prior to the arrival of European colonizers, Uruguay was inhabited by various indigenous groups, each with their own distinct cultures and traditions.

One of the most prominent indigenous groups in Uruguay was the Charrúa people, who inhabited the territory long before the arrival of European settlers. The Charrúas were nomadic hunter-gatherers who roamed the plains of Uruguay, relying on the abundant wildlife for sustenance. They were skilled warriors and fiercely defended their territory against rival indigenous groups and later against European colonizers.

When Spanish explorers first arrived in the region in the early 16th century, they encountered several indigenous tribes, including the Charrúas, Guaraníes, and Guaycurúes. These encounters were often marked by conflict, as the Spanish sought to assert control over the land and its resources.

In the early years of colonization, the Spanish established several settlements along the coast of present-day Uruguay, including Colonia del Sacramento and Montevideo. These settlements served as strategic outposts for trade and military defense, but the harsh conditions and frequent conflicts with indigenous peoples made life difficult for early European settlers.

Despite their best efforts, the Spanish were unable to fully subdue the indigenous populations of Uruguay, who continued to resist colonization through guerrilla warfare and other forms of resistance. The Charrúas, in particular, became legendary for their fierce resistance against European encroachment, and their legacy continues to be celebrated in Uruguay to this day.

As European colonization expanded throughout the region, the indigenous population of Uruguay dwindled due to disease, warfare, and forced assimilation. By the late 19th century, the indigenous population had been largely decimated, and their cultures and traditions were in danger of being lost forever.

Today, efforts are underway to preserve and celebrate Uruguay's indigenous heritage, with initiatives aimed at preserving traditional languages, customs, and artifacts. Museums and cultural centers throughout the country provide insights into the rich history and heritage of Uruguay's indigenous peoples, ensuring that their legacy will endure for generations to come.

Colonial Era: Spanish Influence and Conquest

The Colonial Era in Uruguay marks a significant period in the country's history, characterized by Spanish influence and the conquest of indigenous territories. It begins with the arrival of Spanish explorers in the early 16th century, who were drawn to the riches of the New World and sought to establish colonies in South America.

One of the first European settlements in present-day Uruguay was Colonia del Sacramento, founded by the Portuguese in 1680. However, control of the territory shifted frequently between the Spanish and the Portuguese, leading to centuries of conflict and rivalry over control of the region.

In 1726, the Spanish established the settlement of Montevideo, strategically located along the banks of the Río de la Plata. Montevideo quickly grew into a bustling port city, serving as a gateway for trade and exploration in the region.

The Spanish colonization of Uruguay was driven by a desire for wealth and power, as well as a mission to spread Christianity to the indigenous peoples of the New World. Spanish missionaries played a key role in the colonization process, establishing missions and converting indigenous populations to Christianity.

Despite the efforts of the Spanish to assert control over the territory, they faced resistance from the indigenous peoples of Uruguay, particularly the Charrúas. The Charrúas fiercely defended their land and way of life against European encroachment, leading to frequent conflicts and skirmishes throughout the colonial period.

The colonial era also saw the establishment of the encomienda system, in which Spanish settlers were granted control over indigenous labor and resources in exchange for loyalty to the crown. This system was exploitative and oppressive, leading to widespread abuses of indigenous peoples and contributing to the decline of their populations.

Throughout the colonial period, Uruguay remained a remote and sparsely populated frontier on the fringes of the Spanish Empire. The harsh conditions and constant threat of indigenous resistance made life difficult for European settlers, who struggled to establish permanent settlements in the region.

Despite these challenges, the Spanish presence in Uruguay laid the foundations for the country's cultural and political identity. Spanish language, religion, and customs became deeply ingrained in Uruguayan society, shaping the country's development for centuries to come.

Independence and Nation Building: Uruguay's Road to Sovereignty

The road to independence and nation-building in Uruguay was a tumultuous journey marked by political upheaval, social unrest, and armed conflict. Uruguay's quest for sovereignty began in the early 19th century, as revolutionary fervor swept across Latin America and fueled calls for independence from Spanish colonial rule.

In 1811, inspired by the revolutionary movements in neighboring countries, Uruguayans rose up against Spanish colonial authorities, sparking the Uruguay War of Independence. Led by figures such as José Gervasio Artigas, a national hero and leader of the independence movement, Uruguayan revolutionaries fought bravely against Spanish forces in a bid to secure their freedom.

The struggle for independence was not without its challenges, as internal divisions and external pressures threatened to derail the fledgling nation's aspirations. Uruguay's strategic location between Argentina and Brazil made it a battleground for competing regional powers, leading to decades of instability and conflict.

After years of fighting, Uruguay finally declared its independence from Spain in 1825, following a diplomatic and military campaign supported by both Argentina and Brazil. However, the newly independent nation soon found itself embroiled in a bitter struggle for control between rival factions vying for power and influence.

The period following independence was characterized by political instability and civil strife, as competing factions fought for control of the country's government and resources. The struggle for power culminated in the brutal Uruguayan Civil War of the 1830s, which pitted the forces of the Colorados against the Blancos in a bloody conflict that left thousands dead and the country deeply divided.

Despite the challenges and setbacks, Uruguay eventually emerged from the turmoil of the early 19th century as a sovereign and independent nation. In 1830, the country adopted its first constitution and established a republican form of government, laying the foundations for modern Uruguayan society.

The years that followed saw Uruguay embark on a path of nation-building and development, as efforts were made to consolidate political stability, promote economic growth, and foster social cohesion. The country's commitment to democracy and pluralism helped to solidify its status as one of the most stable and prosperous nations in Latin America.

Today, Uruguay stands as a testament to the resilience and determination of its people, who overcame adversity to forge a nation that is proud, prosperous, and free. The road to sovereignty was long and arduous, but Uruguay's journey serves as an inspiration to nations around the world striving to build a better future for themselves and their citizens.

The Era of Dictatorship and Democratic Transition

The era of dictatorship and democratic transition in Uruguay represents a turbulent period in the country's history, marked by political repression, human rights abuses, and the eventual restoration of democracy. Following decades of political instability and economic hardship, Uruguay fell under the grip of military dictatorship in 1973, when the armed forces seized power in a coup d'état.

Under the rule of the military junta, civil liberties were curtailed, political opposition was suppressed, and thousands of Uruguayans were detained, tortured, or disappeared. The regime justified its actions as necessary to combat left-wing guerrilla groups and restore order to the country.

However, the harsh repression of dissent only served to deepen divisions within Uruguayan society and fuel resistance to military rule. Throughout the dictatorship, brave individuals and organizations continued to speak out against human rights abuses and advocate for democracy, often at great personal risk.

One of the most notorious aspects of the dictatorship was the systematic use of torture and other forms of state-sponsored violence against political opponents. The notorious clandestine detention centers, such as the Automotores Orletti in Buenos Aires, became symbols of the regime's brutality and disregard for human rights.

Despite the regime's efforts to suppress dissent, opposition to military rule continued to grow both domestically and internationally. In the late 1970s and early 1980s, Uruguayans took to the streets in mass protests demanding an end to dictatorship and the restoration of democracy.

In response to mounting pressure, the military junta agreed to hold elections in 1984, marking the beginning of Uruguay's transition to democracy. The elections were won by the center-right Colorado Party, and Julio María Sanguinetti was inaugurated as president, signaling a new chapter in Uruguay's history.

The transition to democracy was not without its challenges, as the country grappled with the legacy of dictatorship and the need to address past human rights abuses. In the years that followed, Uruguayans worked tirelessly to build democratic institutions, strengthen the rule of law, and promote reconciliation and justice.

Today, Uruguay is widely regarded as one of the most stable and democratic countries in Latin America, with strong institutions, a vibrant civil society, and a commitment to human rights. The era of dictatorship and democratic transition serves as a reminder of the importance of safeguarding democracy and respecting the rights and dignity of all individuals, even in the face of adversity.

Uruguay's Political System: Understanding its Democratic Framework

Understanding Uruguay's political system is essential to grasping the country's democratic framework and governance structure. Uruguay operates as a representative democratic republic, with a multi-party system and separation of powers among the executive, legislative, and judicial branches.

At the heart of Uruguay's political system is the presidency, which serves as the head of state and government. The president is elected to a five-year term through a two-round voting system, with candidates needing to secure an absolute majority in the first round or face a runoff election between the top two candidates.

The executive branch, led by the president, holds significant powers, including the authority to appoint ministers, propose legislation, and oversee the implementation of government policies. The president is also the commander-in-chief of the armed forces and represents Uruguay in diplomatic affairs on the international stage.

The legislative branch of Uruguay is bicameral, consisting of the Chamber of Deputies and the Senate. The Chamber of Deputies is composed of 99 members elected by proportional representation, while the Senate has 30 members elected to represent each of Uruguay's 19 departments. Both chambers are responsible for enacting laws, approving the national budget, and overseeing government actions.

Uruguay's political landscape is characterized by a multiparty system, with several political parties vying for power and representation in government. The two main political parties are the center-right Colorado Party and the center-left Broad Front, which have historically been the dominant forces in Uruguayan politics.

In addition to the executive and legislative branches, Uruguay has an independent judiciary tasked with interpreting and upholding the constitution and laws of the country. The Supreme Court of Justice is the highest judicial authority in Uruguay, responsible for ensuring the rule of law and protecting citizens' rights.

Uruguay's political system is also notable for its commitment to democracy, with regular free and fair elections, respect for human rights, and a strong tradition of civil liberties. The country's democratic framework has been tested and strengthened over time, with Uruguayans actively participating in the political process through voting, advocacy, and civic engagement.

Overall, understanding Uruguay's political system provides insight into the country's governance structure, democratic principles, and commitment to upholding the rule of law. By navigating the complexities of its political institutions and processes, one can gain a deeper appreciation for Uruguay's vibrant democracy and the values it represents.

Economy and Trade: Navigating Uruguay's Economic Landscape

Navigating Uruguay's economic landscape offers insights into the country's diverse economic sectors, trade relationships, and challenges. Uruguay boasts a mixed economy, characterized by a blend of agriculture, services, and industry, with a strong emphasis on international trade.

Agriculture has historically been a cornerstone of Uruguay's economy, with the country's fertile land and temperate climate supporting the production of a wide range of agricultural products. Uruguay is one of the world's leading producers of beef, wool, and soybeans, with livestock farming playing a significant role in rural livelihoods and export earnings.

In addition to agriculture, Uruguay's services sector is a vital component of the economy, encompassing finance, tourism, telecommunications, and professional services. The country's strategic location, stable political environment, and well-developed infrastructure make it an attractive destination for foreign investment and business expansion.

Uruguay has also made significant strides in industrial development, with manufacturing contributing to economic growth and diversification. The automotive, chemical, and pharmaceutical industries are among the key sectors driving

Uruguay's industrial output, supported by government incentives and investment in innovation and technology.

International trade plays a crucial role in Uruguay's economy, with the country actively participating in global markets and trade agreements. Uruguay is a member of Mercosur, a regional trade bloc comprising Argentina, Brazil, Paraguay, and Venezuela, which promotes economic integration and cooperation among its member states.

Uruguay has also pursued bilateral trade agreements with countries outside of Mercosur, seeking to expand market access and diversify its export destinations. The United States, China, and the European Union are among Uruguay's top trading partners, with exports including agricultural products, textiles, and manufactured goods.

Despite its economic strengths, Uruguay faces challenges such as income inequality, unemployment, and fiscal sustainability. The government has implemented social welfare programs and economic reforms aimed at addressing these issues and promoting inclusive growth.

Overall, navigating Uruguay's economic landscape requires an understanding of its diverse economic sectors, trade relationships, and policy priorities. By embracing innovation, fostering entrepreneurship, and promoting sustainable development, Uruguay aims to build a resilient economy that benefits all its citizens.

Social Welfare and Education: Pillars of Uruguayan Society

Social welfare and education stand as pillars of Uruguayan society, reflecting the country's commitment to equity, inclusivity, and human development. Uruguay has long been recognized for its progressive social policies and robust education system, which aim to ensure that all citizens have access to quality healthcare, education, and social services.

The Uruguayan government has implemented various social welfare programs aimed at alleviating poverty, reducing inequality, and improving the overall well-being of its citizens. These programs include cash transfers, food assistance, and healthcare subsidies, which help to support vulnerable populations and promote social inclusion.

One of the most notable social welfare initiatives in Uruguay is the National Integrated Health System (SNIS), which provides universal access to healthcare services for all citizens. Under the SNIS, healthcare is funded through a combination of public and private contributions, with a focus on preventive care, primary healthcare, and equitable access to medical services.

Uruguay's commitment to education is equally impressive, with a strong emphasis on universal access to quality education from early childhood through higher education. The country boasts a high literacy rate and a well-developed public education system that provides free and compulsory education for all children up to the age of 18.

In addition to traditional schooling, Uruguay has implemented innovative education reforms aimed at enhancing learning outcomes and promoting educational equity. One such initiative is the Plan Ceibal, which provides all primary and secondary school students with free laptops and internet access, enabling them to access educational resources and digital learning tools.

Uruguay's investment in education extends beyond the classroom, with a focus on lifelong learning and skill development. The country offers a range of vocational training programs, adult education courses, and continuing education opportunities to help individuals acquire new skills and adapt to changing economic realities.

Furthermore, Uruguay recognizes the importance of early childhood development in shaping future outcomes, investing in programs that promote early childhood education, nutrition, and healthcare. These initiatives aim to provide children with the foundation they need to thrive academically, socially, and emotionally.

Overall, social welfare and education are integral components of Uruguayan society, reflecting the country's values of equity, solidarity, and social justice. By investing in the well-being and education of its citizens, Uruguay aims to build a more inclusive and prosperous society for generations to come.

Uruguayan Wildlife: From Pampas to Coastline

Uruguay's wildlife spans diverse ecosystems, ranging from the expansive pampas to the pristine coastline, offering a rich tapestry of biodiversity to explore. In the vast grasslands of the pampas, visitors can encounter a variety of wildlife species, including the iconic gauchos and their cattle herds. These vast plains are home to numerous bird species, such as the rhea, a flightless bird similar to the ostrich, and the colorful Southern lapwing.

Moving towards Uruguay's coastline, one encounters a different array of wildlife adapted to the coastal environment. Along the sandy beaches and rocky shores, visitors may spot colonies of South American sea lions basking in the sun or playful pods of dolphins frolicking in the waves. Offshore, the nutrient-rich waters of the Atlantic Ocean support a diverse marine ecosystem, including various species of fish, sharks, and seabirds.

In the wetlands and marshes of Uruguay, visitors can observe an abundance of birdlife, including herons, ibises, and flamingos, which flock to these habitats in search of food and shelter. The Bañados del Este Biosphere Reserve, located near the city of Rocha, is a prime birdwatching destination, offering opportunities to see rare and endangered species in their natural habitat.

Uruguay's forests and woodlands are also home to a variety of wildlife, including mammals such as capybaras, armadillos, and howler monkeys. The country's interior is dotted with national parks and protected areas, where visitors can explore pristine wilderness and observe native flora and fauna in their natural environment.

Conservation efforts in Uruguay aim to protect and preserve the country's unique wildlife and habitats for future generations. National parks, reserves, and protected areas play a crucial role in safeguarding biodiversity and promoting sustainable development. Additionally, educational programs and ecotourism initiatives help raise awareness about the importance of conservation and foster appreciation for Uruguay's natural heritage.

Overall, Uruguay's wildlife offers a glimpse into the country's natural beauty and ecological diversity. Whether exploring the vast grasslands of the interior or the rugged coastline along the Atlantic Ocean, visitors are sure to encounter a wide array of fascinating wildlife species that call Uruguay home.

Gastronomy Delights: Exploring Uruguayan Cuisine

Exploring Uruguayan cuisine unveils a delightful fusion of flavors, influenced by the country's cultural heritage and natural abundance. At the heart of Uruguayan gastronomy lies a love for grilled meats, particularly beef, which is central to the traditional dish known as "asado." Asado is a social event as much as a meal, where friends and family gather around the grill to enjoy various cuts of beef, sausages, and offal cooked to perfection over open flames.

Accompanying the grilled meats are an array of side dishes that showcase Uruguay's agricultural bounty. These may include salads, grilled vegetables, and chimichurri sauce, a tangy condiment made from parsley, garlic, vinegar, and spices. Another staple of Uruguayan cuisine is the "choripán," a simple yet satisfying sandwich consisting of grilled chorizo sausage served on crusty bread with chimichurri sauce.

Seafood also plays a prominent role in Uruguayan cuisine, thanks to the country's extensive coastline and rich marine resources. Locally caught fish and shellfish feature prominently in dishes such as "chivito al mar," a hearty seafood stew made with a variety of fish, shrimp, and squid, simmered in a savory broth with vegetables and spices.

In addition to grilled meats and seafood, Uruguayan cuisine boasts a diverse array of pastries, breads, and desserts influenced by European immigrants. "Bizcochos," or sweet pastries, are a popular breakfast or snack item, often enjoyed with a cup of "mate," Uruguay's national beverage. Other sweet treats include "alfajores," delicate cookies filled with dulce de leche, and "chaja," a sponge cake layered with whipped cream and peaches.

Uruguayan cuisine also reflects the country's agricultural heritage, with dishes featuring locally grown fruits and vegetables such as potatoes, pumpkins, and citrus fruits. These ingredients are often used to create hearty stews, soups, and casseroles, which are enjoyed year-round, particularly during the cooler months.

Overall, exploring Uruguayan cuisine offers a delicious journey through the country's cultural traditions, culinary innovations, and natural bounty. From sizzling steaks on the grill to sweet pastries and desserts, Uruguayan gastronomy delights the senses and celebrates the richness of the country's culinary heritage.

Mate: The National Beverage and Cultural Icon

Mate holds a special place in the hearts and culture of Uruguay, serving not just as a beverage but as a symbol of friendship, community, and tradition. Originating from indigenous cultures in South America, mate is made from the leaves of the yerba mate plant, which are dried, ground, and steeped in hot water to create a flavorful infusion.

The tradition of drinking mate dates back centuries, with indigenous peoples using gourds and hollowed-out calabash fruits as vessels for drinking the infusion. Today, mate is typically consumed using a special gourd called a "mate" or "mate cup," along with a metal straw known as a "bombilla." The ritual of preparing and sharing mate has become an integral part of Uruguayan social life, with friends, families, and colleagues gathering to share mate throughout the day.

The cultural significance of mate extends beyond its role as a beverage, encompassing themes of hospitality, camaraderie, and identity. Sharing mate is considered a gesture of friendship and goodwill, with participants forming a "circle of friendship" as they pass the gourd from person to person. The act of sharing mate fosters a sense of closeness and connection among individuals, transcending social barriers and fostering a sense of belonging.

In addition to its social significance, mate is also valued for its health benefits and energizing properties. Rich in antioxidants, vitamins, and minerals, mate is believed to boost energy, aid digestion, and improve mental clarity. It is often consumed as a morning pick-me-up or as a refreshing beverage throughout the day.

Mate is deeply ingrained in Uruguayan culture, with customs and rituals surrounding its preparation and consumption passed down through generations. Special etiquette governs the sharing of mate, with rules dictating the order in which participants drink from the gourd and the proper way to pass it to the next person.

During Uruguay's National Day of the Mate, held annually on December 1st, the country celebrates its cultural heritage and the importance of mate in Uruguayan society. Festivals, competitions, and cultural events showcase the art of mate-making, with participants coming together to share stories, traditions, and of course, plenty of mate.

Overall, mate embodies the spirit of Uruguay, encapsulating the values of friendship, community, and tradition that are cherished by its people. As a national beverage and cultural icon, mate continues to play a central role in the lives of Uruguayans, bringing people together and nurturing bonds that transcend time and place.

Montevideo: Uruguay's Vibrant Capital City

Montevideo, Uruguay's vibrant capital city, is a bustling metropolis situated on the country's southern coast. With a population of over 1.3 million people, Montevideo is the cultural, political, and economic hub of Uruguay, renowned for its rich history, diverse architecture, and vibrant cultural scene.

The city's history dates back to the early colonial period, when Spanish settlers established the settlement of Montevideo in the early 18th century. Over the centuries, Montevideo grew into a major port city, serving as a vital hub for trade and commerce in the region. Today, the Port of Montevideo remains one of the busiest ports in South America, handling millions of tons of cargo each year.

Montevideo's architecture reflects its diverse cultural heritage, with influences ranging from Spanish colonial to Art Deco and modernist styles. The historic Ciudad Vieja (Old City) is home to charming cobblestone streets, colonial-era buildings, and historic landmarks such as the Plaza Independencia and the Solis Theatre, Uruguay's oldest theater.

In addition to its historic charm, Montevideo boasts a thriving cultural scene, with numerous museums, galleries, theaters, and music venues showcasing the country's artistic heritage. The National Museum of Visual Arts, the National History Museum, and the Juan Manuel Blanes Museum are just a few of the cultural institutions that attract visitors from around the world.

Montevideo is also known for its vibrant street art scene, with colorful murals and graffiti adorning buildings and walls throughout the city. Street art festivals and exhibitions are held regularly, highlighting the work of local and international artists and adding to the city's dynamic urban landscape.

One of the defining features of Montevideo is its stunning coastline, which stretches for miles along the Rio de la Plata. The city's waterfront promenade, known as the Rambla, offers breathtaking views of the river and serves as a popular gathering spot for locals and tourists alike.

Montevideo's culinary scene is equally diverse, with a wide range of restaurants, cafes, and markets offering everything from traditional Uruguayan cuisine to international fare. Visitors can sample local specialties such as chivito (a hearty sandwich), empanadas (stuffed pastries), and of course, Uruguayan beef cooked to perfection on the grill.

Overall, Montevideo captivates visitors with its unique blend of history, culture, and natural beauty. From its historic landmarks and vibrant neighborhoods to its lively cultural scene and mouthwatering cuisine, Uruguay's capital city offers a wealth of experiences waiting to be explored.

Colonia del Sacramento: A Glimpse into Uruguay's Colonial Past

Colonia del Sacramento offers a captivating glimpse into Uruguay's colonial past, with its well-preserved historic quarter and charming cobblestone streets evoking the spirit of a bygone era. Founded by the Portuguese in 1680, Colonia del Sacramento is one of the oldest cities in Uruguay and holds UNESCO World Heritage status for its cultural significance.

The city's strategic location along the banks of the Rio de la Plata made it a coveted prize for European powers vying for control of the region. Throughout its history, Colonia del Sacramento changed hands multiple times between the Spanish and the Portuguese, resulting in a rich tapestry of architectural styles and cultural influences.

The historic quarter of Colonia del Sacramento is characterized by its colonial-era buildings, many of which have been lovingly restored and preserved. Visitors can wander through narrow cobblestone streets lined with colorful houses, visit quaint cafes and boutiques, and explore historic landmarks such as the Portuguese Museum and the Matriz Church.

One of the most iconic features of Colonia del Sacramento is its picturesque waterfront, where visitors can stroll along the promenade and enjoy stunning views of the Rio de la Plata. The city's waterfront also boasts a number of historic sites, including the remnants of the city's old fortifications and the iconic lighthouse, which offers panoramic views of the surrounding area.

Colonia del Sacramento is also known for its rich cultural heritage, with festivals, events, and exhibitions celebrating the city's colonial past and vibrant cultural scene. The city's annual Fiesta de la Vendimia, or Grape Harvest Festival, showcases Uruguay's wine-making tradition and features wine tastings, live music, and cultural performances.

In addition to its historic and cultural attractions, Colonia del Sacramento offers visitors opportunities for outdoor recreation and relaxation. The city's surrounding countryside is dotted with vineyards, olive groves, and citrus orchards, where visitors can sample local wines, olive oils, and citrus fruits.

Overall, Colonia del Sacramento is a treasure trove of history, culture, and natural beauty, offering visitors a unique glimpse into Uruguay's colonial past and a tranquil escape from the hustle and bustle of modern life. Whether exploring its historic streets, enjoying its waterfront views, or savoring its culinary delights, Colonia del Sacramento captivates visitors with its timeless charm and allure.

Punta del Este: Playground of the Rich and Famous

Punta del Este, often dubbed the "Playground of the Rich and Famous," is a glamorous seaside resort city located on Uruguay's southeastern coast. Renowned for its stunning beaches, upscale resorts, and vibrant nightlife, Punta del Este attracts jet-setters, celebrities, and affluent travelers from around the world.

The city's reputation as a luxury destination dates back to the mid-20th century when it became a favorite retreat for wealthy Argentinians and Uruguayans seeking sun, sea, and sophistication. Since then, Punta del Este has evolved into an international hotspot for high-end tourism, drawing visitors with its blend of natural beauty and exclusive amenities.

Punta del Este's pristine beaches are among its most alluring attractions, offering miles of golden sand and crystal-clear waters ideal for swimming, sunbathing, and water sports. Playa Brava and Playa Mansa are two of the most popular beaches, each with its own unique charm and character.

In addition to its beaches, Punta del Este boasts a wealth of luxury accommodations, including five-star hotels, boutique resorts, and private villas. Many of these establishments offer world-class amenities such as spa facilities, gourmet restaurants, and infinity pools overlooking the ocean, catering to the discerning tastes of affluent travelers.

Punta del Este's nightlife scene is equally legendary, with a plethora of chic bars, nightclubs, and casinos where visitors can see and be seen. During the summer months, the city comes alive with parties, concerts, and cultural events, attracting an eclectic mix of international celebrities, socialites, and trendsetters.

Beyond its beaches and nightlife, Punta del Este offers a range of leisure and recreational activities for visitors to enjoy. Golf enthusiasts can tee off at one of the city's championship golf courses, while yachting enthusiasts can explore the coastline aboard luxury vessels or charter boats.

For those seeking cultural enrichment, Punta del Este is home to several art galleries, museums, and cultural centers showcasing both local and international artists. The city's iconic sculpture park, known as "La Mano" or "The Hand," features a series of massive hand sculptures emerging from the sand, created by Chilean artist Mario Irarrázabal.

Overall, Punta del Este exudes an aura of luxury, exclusivity, and glamour, making it a magnet for the rich and famous seeking an idyllic retreat by the sea. With its stunning beaches, upscale accommodations, and vibrant social scene, Punta del Este remains one of South America's most coveted destinations for those who appreciate the finer things in life.

Ciudad Vieja: Unveiling Montevideo's Historic Heart

Ciudad Vieja, or the Old City, lies at the heart of Montevideo, Uruguay's vibrant capital. Steeped in history and brimming with charm, this historic neighborhood offers a captivating glimpse into Montevideo's colonial past and cultural heritage. Founded in the early 18th century by Spanish settlers, Ciudad Vieja is the oldest part of Montevideo, boasting a rich architectural legacy that reflects its diverse cultural influences.

Wandering through the narrow cobblestone streets of Ciudad Vieja, visitors are transported back in time, surrounded by colonial-era buildings, historic landmarks, and hidden courtyards. The neighborhood's eclectic mix of architectural styles includes Spanish colonial, Art Deco, and neoclassical influences, with ornate facades, wrought-iron balconies, and colorful murals adorning its streets.

One of the most iconic landmarks in Ciudad Vieja is the Plaza Independencia, a bustling square that serves as the gateway to the neighborhood. At the center of the plaza stands a towering statue of Uruguay's national hero, José Artigas, surrounded by historic buildings, monuments, and cultural institutions.

The Ciudad Vieja is also home to a vibrant arts and culture scene, with numerous galleries, museums, and theaters showcasing the works of local and international artists. The Solis Theatre, Uruguay's oldest theater, is located in Ciudad Vieja and hosts a variety of performances, from opera and ballet to theater and concerts.

In addition to its cultural attractions, Ciudad Vieja is a hub for dining, shopping, and entertainment, with a wide range of restaurants, cafes, boutiques, and bars lining its streets. Visitors can sample traditional Uruguayan cuisine, browse artisanal crafts, or sip on a coffee while soaking in the neighborhood's historic ambiance.

Despite its historic charm, Ciudad Vieja has undergone significant revitalization efforts in recent years, with restoration projects aimed at preserving its architectural heritage and improving infrastructure. The neighborhood has experienced a resurgence in popularity, attracting residents, businesses, and tourists eager to experience its unique blend of history and modernity.

Overall, Ciudad Vieja stands as a testament to Montevideo's rich cultural heritage and enduring spirit. Whether exploring its historic streets, admiring its architectural treasures, or immersing oneself in its vibrant atmosphere, Ciudad Vieja offers a captivating journey through time and a window into Uruguay's past.

Salto: Gateway to Uruguay's Northern Region

Salto, situated in the northern region of Uruguay, serves as a gateway to the country's diverse landscapes, cultural heritage, and natural wonders. As one of Uruguay's largest cities, Salto boasts a rich history, vibrant cultural scene, and strategic location along the Uruguay River, which forms the border with Argentina.

The city of Salto is known for its thermal springs, which have been attracting visitors seeking relaxation and rejuvenation for centuries. These natural hot springs are said to have therapeutic properties, with mineral-rich waters that are believed to promote health and well-being. Visitors to Salto can indulge in spa treatments, soak in thermal pools, and enjoy scenic views of the surrounding countryside.

In addition to its thermal springs, Salto is surrounded by fertile farmland and lush greenery, making it a haven for outdoor enthusiasts and nature lovers. The nearby Salto Grande Dam, one of Uruguay's largest hydroelectric power plants, offers opportunities for hiking, fishing, and birdwatching in its expansive reservoir.

Salto is also steeped in history, with architectural landmarks and cultural attractions that reflect its colonial past and indigenous heritage. The city's historic center is home to charming plazas, churches, and museums, including the Salto History Museum and the Cathedral of San Juan Bautista, which dates back to the 19th century.

The region surrounding Salto is known for its agricultural production, particularly citrus fruits, grapes, and livestock. Visitors can explore local farms, orchards, and vineyards, sampling fresh produce and regional specialties such as citrus juices, wines, and cheeses.

In recent years, Salto has emerged as a center for eco-tourism and adventure travel, with opportunities for hiking, horseback riding, and river rafting in the nearby countryside. The city also hosts cultural events, festivals, and exhibitions throughout the year, celebrating its heritage and promoting local arts and crafts.

Overall, Salto offers visitors a unique blend of natural beauty, cultural richness, and outdoor recreation, making it an ideal destination for those looking to explore Uruguay's northern region. Whether soaking in thermal springs, exploring historic landmarks, or venturing into the countryside, Salto invites travelers to experience the best that Uruguay has to offer.

Artigas: Birthplace of Uruguay's National Hero

Artigas, the birthplace of Uruguay's national hero José Gervasio Artigas, holds a special significance in the country's history and cultural identity. Located in the northwest region of Uruguay, near the border with Argentina, Artigas is a small city with a big legacy, honoring the memory of one of Uruguay's most revered figures.

José Gervasio Artigas, often referred to as the "Father of Uruguayan Independence," played a crucial role in leading Uruguay to freedom from Spanish colonial rule in the early 19th century. Born in 1764 in what was then known as Villa de San Carlos, Artigas grew up in a time of political unrest and social upheaval, witnessing firsthand the injustices and inequalities of Spanish colonial rule.

From an early age, Artigas showed a keen interest in politics and social justice, advocating for the rights of the common people and challenging the authority of the Spanish crown. As a military leader, he organized resistance movements and guerrilla campaigns against Spanish forces, earning a reputation as a fearless and charismatic leader.

Artigas's crowning achievement came in 1811 when he led the revolution that resulted in Uruguay's declaration of independence from Spain. He went on to serve as the country's first head of state, drafting its first constitution and laying the foundation for a democratic and egalitarian society.

Today, Artigas is revered as a national hero in Uruguay, with his legacy celebrated through monuments, memorials, and public holidays. The city of Artigas, formerly known as San Carlos, was renamed in his honor in 1915, cementing his place in the country's history and culture.

Visitors to Artigas can explore landmarks and sites associated with Artigas's life and legacy, including his childhood home, the Plaza Artigas, and the Artigas Mausoleum, where his remains are interred. The city also hosts cultural events, exhibitions, and festivals commemorating Artigas's contributions to Uruguay's independence and identity.

In addition to its historical significance, Artigas is known for its scenic beauty, with lush green landscapes, rolling hills, and pristine rivers that attract nature lovers and outdoor enthusiasts. The region is also renowned for its agriculture, particularly cattle farming and citrus production, which contribute to Uruguay's economy and culinary heritage.

Overall, Artigas stands as a symbol of Uruguay's resilience, determination, and quest for freedom, honoring the legacy of José Gervasio Artigas and inspiring future generations to uphold the values of independence, democracy, and social justice.

Uruguay's Football Legacy: A National Passion

Uruguay's football legacy runs deep, ingrained in the fabric of the nation's culture and identity. Since its introduction to Uruguay in the late 19th century, football has captured the hearts and minds of Uruguayans, becoming more than just a sport but a national passion.

The roots of Uruguay's football obsession can be traced back to the early days of the game's development in South America. In 1900, the first football club in Uruguay, Albion Football Club, was founded in Montevideo, laying the groundwork for the country's future dominance in the sport.

Uruguay's rise to football prominence culminated in the 1920s and 1930s when the national team achieved unprecedented success on the international stage. In 1930, Uruguay hosted and won the inaugural FIFA World Cup, defeating Argentina in the final to claim the title of world champions. This historic victory cemented Uruguay's status as a football powerhouse and solidified its place in the annals of football history.

The success of the Uruguayan national team inspired generations of young players and instilled a sense of pride and patriotism in the country's footballing tradition. The national team, known as "La Celeste" (The Sky Blue), has continued to enjoy success in subsequent World Cups, winning the tournament for a second time in 1950 and consistently performing well in regional competitions such as the Copa América.

In addition to its achievements on the international stage, Uruguayan football is renowned for its rich talent pool and distinctive playing style. Uruguayans are known for their passion, skill, and tenacity on the field, with a strong emphasis on teamwork, discipline, and tactical awareness.

At the club level, Uruguayan football is dominated by two rival teams, Club Nacional de Football and Club Atlético Peñarol, both based in Montevideo. These clubs boast storied histories and fierce rivalries, with matches between them, known as the "Clásico del Fútbol Uruguayo," drawing passionate crowds and intense competition.

Football is more than just a sport in Uruguay; it is a source of national pride, unity, and identity. From the streets of Montevideo to the rural communities of the interior, football is woven into the fabric of everyday life, bringing people together and transcending social, economic, and cultural divides.

Uruguay's football legacy is a testament to the country's resilience, determination, and unwavering spirit. It is a legacy that continues to inspire and unite Uruguayans, both at home and abroad, as they celebrate their rich footballing tradition and look to the future with optimism and pride.

Carnival in Uruguay: Festive Celebrations and Cultural Pride

Carnival in Uruguay is not just a celebration; it's a vibrant expression of the country's cultural heritage and communal spirit. This annual festival, held in the weeks leading up to Lent, is a time of joy, music, and revelry that brings together people of all ages and backgrounds to celebrate life and creativity.

The roots of Carnival in Uruguay can be traced back to the country's European and African influences, blending Catholic traditions with African rhythms and dances brought over by enslaved Africans. Over time, Carnival evolved into a uniquely Uruguayan celebration, characterized by colorful parades, elaborate costumes, and lively street parties.

The heart of Carnival in Uruguay beats strongest in Montevideo, the capital city, where the festivities reach a fever pitch with the Desfile de Llamadas, or Parade of Calls. This iconic event features drum ensembles, dancers, and floats parading through the streets of the Barrio Sur and Palermo neighborhoods, accompanied by the pulsating rhythms of candombe music.

Candombe, a traditional Afro-Uruguayan music and dance genre, lies at the heart of Carnival celebrations in Uruguay. Originating from African rhythms brought by slaves to Uruguay, candombe is characterized by its rhythmic drumming, syncopated beats, and vibrant choreography. During Carnival, candombe groups known as comparsas take to the streets, filling the air with the infectious sounds of drums and chanting as they dance their way through the crowds.

In addition to the Desfile de Llamadas, Carnival in Uruguay features a variety of other events and activities, including murga performances, carnival balls, and neighborhood street parties known as "tablados." Murga, a form of musical theater with roots in Spanish and Italian traditions, combines music, dance, and satire to entertain and engage audiences during Carnival.

One of the most beloved traditions of Carnival in Uruguay is the choosing of the Carnival Queen, or "Reina del Carnaval," who represents the spirit and beauty of the festival. The selection process involves elaborate competitions and pageants, with contestants vying for the title through talent showcases, interviews, and public appearances.

Carnival in Uruguay is not only a time of celebration but also a reflection of the country's cultural diversity and social dynamics. It is a celebration of inclusion, tolerance, and community, where people from all walks of life come together to revel in the joy of Carnival and honor the rich tapestry of Uruguayan culture.

Overall, Carnival in Uruguay is a testament to the country's creativity, resilience, and joie de vivre. It is a time to set aside differences, embrace diversity, and celebrate the shared values that unite Uruguayans as they dance, sing, and rejoice in the spirit of Carnival.

Tango and Candombe: Musical Traditions of Uruguay

Tango and Candombe stand as two pillars of Uruguay's rich musical heritage, each with its own unique history, rhythms, and cultural significance. Tango, often associated with neighboring Argentina, also holds a special place in Uruguayan culture, particularly in the capital city of Montevideo, where it has flourished alongside other musical genres.

Tango first arrived in Uruguay in the late 19th century, brought over by European immigrants, particularly from Italy and Spain. In the bustling port city of Montevideo, tango found fertile ground for growth and innovation, blending with local musical traditions to create a distinct Uruguayan style. While Buenos Aires may be considered the birthplace of tango, Montevideo played a crucial role in its development and popularization.

Today, Montevideo boasts a vibrant tango scene, with numerous milongas (tango dance halls), tango clubs, and live music venues where enthusiasts can dance the night away to the soulful melodies and intricate rhythms of this iconic genre. Tango festivals, workshops, and competitions are held throughout the year, attracting dancers and musicians from around the world.

Candombe, on the other hand, is a uniquely Afro-Uruguayan musical tradition that traces its roots back to the African diaspora and the era of slavery in Uruguay. Originating from the rhythms and dances brought over by enslaved Africans, candombe evolved into a vibrant cultural expression that remains an integral part of Uruguayan identity.

Candombe is characterized by its rhythmic drumming, syncopated beats, and lively choreography, with groups of drummers known as comparsas taking to the streets during Carnival and other festive occasions to perform and celebrate. The sound of candombe drums reverberating through the streets is a quintessential part of Uruguay's cultural landscape, symbolizing resilience, community, and cultural pride.

In addition to tango and candombe, Uruguay is also home to a diverse array of musical genres and traditions, reflecting the country's multicultural heritage and cosmopolitan identity. From traditional folk music such as murga and payada to modern styles like rock, jazz, and electronic music, Uruguay's musical landscape is as eclectic as it is vibrant.

Overall, tango and candombe represent two distinct but interconnected threads in the rich tapestry of Uruguayan culture. Whether dancing to the passionate rhythms of tango or drumming to the infectious beats of candombe, Uruguayans embrace music as a form of expression, connection, and celebration, weaving together the diverse influences that make up their musical identity.

Gaucho Culture: Exploring Uruguay's Cowboy Heritage

Uruguay's Gaucho culture epitomizes the rugged spirit and frontier heritage of the country's rural communities. Derived from the Spanish word for cowboy, "gauchos" have long been integral to Uruguay's agricultural and livestock industries, shaping the country's identity and folklore.

The origins of Gaucho culture in Uruguay can be traced back to the 18th and 19th centuries when Spanish colonizers introduced cattle ranching to the region. Uruguay's vast grasslands, known as the pampas, provided ideal conditions for cattle grazing, and gauchos emerged as skilled horsemen and cattle herders, adept at navigating the rugged terrain.

Gauchos were known for their independence, resourcefulness, and rugged lifestyle, living off the land and roaming the countryside in search of work and adventure. Clad in distinctive attire, including wide-brimmed hats, ponchos, and bombachas (baggy trousers), gauchos became iconic figures in Uruguayan folklore, celebrated in literature, music, and art.

One of the defining characteristics of Gaucho culture is the mate, a traditional South American drink made from steeped yerba mate leaves. Mate holds a special place in Uruguayan culture, serving as a symbol of hospitality, friendship, and communal bonding among gauchos and rural communities.

In addition to their role as cattle herders, gauchos played a vital role in Uruguay's struggle for independence from Spanish colonial rule. Many gauchos joined the fight for freedom, serving as guerrilla fighters and cavalry soldiers in battles against Spanish forces.

Today, Gaucho culture remains alive and well in Uruguay, particularly in rural areas where traditional customs and practices are preserved and celebrated. Each year, the country hosts a variety of gaucho festivals and rodeo events, showcasing horsemanship, cattle herding skills, and traditional gaucho attire.

The legacy of Gaucho culture extends beyond rural life, influencing various aspects of Uruguayan society, including cuisine, music, and language. Traditional gaucho dishes such as asado (barbecue) and chivito (grilled meat sandwich) are staples of Uruguayan cuisine, while folk music genres such as payada and milonga draw inspiration from gaucho traditions.

Overall, Gaucho culture is an integral part of Uruguay's national identity, embodying the spirit of resilience, independence, and rugged individualism that defines the country's rural heritage. Whether herding cattle on the pampas, sharing mate with friends, or participating in gaucho festivals, Uruguayans continue to embrace and celebrate their cowboy heritage as a source of pride and cultural richness.

Religious Diversity: Christianity and Beyond in Uruguay

Religious diversity in Uruguay reflects the country's commitment to freedom of religion and tolerance. While the majority of Uruguayans identify as Christians, there is a significant presence of non-Christian religions as well.

Christianity, particularly Catholicism, has historically been the dominant religion in Uruguay. Catholicism was introduced to the region by Spanish colonizers in the 16th century and became the official religion during the colonial period. Today, the Catholic Church remains influential in Uruguayan society, with many cultural traditions and holidays rooted in Catholicism.

In addition to Catholicism, Protestantism has gained a foothold in Uruguay, particularly among evangelical and Pentecostal denominations. These Protestant churches have experienced significant growth in recent decades, attracting followers through their emphasis on personal salvation, charismatic worship, and community outreach.

Beyond Christianity, Uruguay is also home to small but vibrant Jewish and Muslim communities. Jewish immigrants began settling in Uruguay in the late 19th century, fleeing persecution in Europe and seeking economic opportunities in South America. Today, Uruguay's Jewish community is relatively small but active, with synagogues, schools, and cultural institutions in cities like Montevideo and Punta del Este.

Similarly, Uruguay's Muslim community traces its roots back to the late 19th century when immigrants from the Middle East and North Africa began arriving in the country. While Muslims make up a small percentage of the population, Uruguay is known for its religious tolerance and acceptance of diverse faiths.

In addition to Christianity, Judaism, and Islam, Uruguay is also home to adherents of other faiths, including Buddhism, Hinduism, and indigenous religions. These minority religions contribute to the country's cultural diversity and enrich the tapestry of religious life in Uruguay.

Overall, Uruguay's commitment to religious freedom and pluralism is reflected in its diverse religious landscape. While Christianity remains the dominant religion, the presence of other faiths underscores Uruguay's tradition of tolerance, respect, and acceptance of religious diversity. As the country continues to evolve, so too does its religious identity, with Uruguayans embracing a variety of beliefs and practices that reflect their individual and collective values.

Uruguayan Literature: Richness in Words and Stories

Uruguayan literature is a testament to the country's cultural richness and literary heritage, encompassing a diverse range of genres, styles, and voices that reflect the complexities of Uruguayan society and history. From the colonial era to the present day, Uruguayan writers have made significant contributions to world literature, capturing the essence of their nation and its people through words and stories.

One of the earliest literary figures in Uruguay was Fray Bartolomé Hidalgo, a priest and poet who lived during the colonial period. Hidalgo is considered one of the pioneers of Spanish-American literature, known for his satirical poems and gaucho-inspired verses that celebrated the rugged frontier life of the pampas.

In the 19th century, Uruguay experienced a literary renaissance, fueled by the country's struggle for independence and burgeoning cultural identity. Writers such as Juan Zorrilla de San Martín and José Enrique Rodó emerged as leading figures of the period, producing works that explored themes of nationhood, identity, and social justice.

One of the most celebrated works of Uruguayan literature is "La cautiva" (The Captive), an epic poem written by Zorrilla de San Martín that tells the story of a young woman kidnapped by indigenous tribes during the colonial era. The poem is considered a masterpiece of Latin American literature, blending historical events with romanticism and myth.

In the early 20th century, Uruguay experienced a literary boom known as the "Generation of 1900," characterized by a renewed interest in social realism and modernist experimentation. Writers such as Horacio Quiroga and Felisberto Hernández emerged as leading voices of the period, exploring themes of nature, madness, and the human condition.

Uruguayan literature continued to flourish in the 20th century, with authors such as Mario Benedetti, Juan Carlos Onetti, and Idea Vilariño gaining international recognition for their innovative and socially engaged writing. Benedetti, in particular, is celebrated for his poetry, short stories, and novels that explore themes of love, exile, and political oppression.

In recent years, Uruguayan literature has continued to evolve, with a new generation of writers exploring contemporary issues such as globalization, urbanization, and identity. Authors such as Claudia Amengual, Cristina Peri Rossi, and Daniel Mella have garnered critical acclaim for their bold and experimental writing styles.

Overall, Uruguayan literature is a reflection of the country's vibrant cultural landscape and its ongoing quest for self-expression and identity. From the epic poems of the colonial era to the avant-garde experiments of the 21st century, Uruguayan writers have left an indelible mark on world literature, enriching the literary canon with their unique perspectives and storytelling prowess.

The Legacy of Jose Gervasio Artigas: Father of Uruguayan Independence

The legacy of José Gervasio Artigas looms large in Uruguayan history, earning him the title of the "Father of Uruguayan Independence" and solidifying his place as one of the country's most revered figures. Born in 1764 in what is now Uruguay, Artigas came of age during a time of political upheaval and social unrest in South America.

Artigas's leadership and military prowess played a crucial role in Uruguay's struggle for independence from Spanish colonial rule in the early 19th century. He organized and led resistance movements against Spanish forces, rallying ordinary citizens and indigenous peoples to fight for freedom and equality.

In 1811, Artigas led the revolution that resulted in Uruguay's declaration of independence from Spain, marking a turning point in the country's history. He went on to serve as the leader of the independent Provincia Oriental, which would later become Uruguay, drafting its first constitution and laying the foundation for a democratic and egalitarian society.

Artigas's vision for Uruguay was one of social justice, decentralization, and grassroots democracy. He advocated for land reform, indigenous rights, and the empowerment of ordinary citizens, earning him the loyalty and admiration of the rural poor and marginalized communities.

Despite his contributions to Uruguay's independence, Artigas's legacy was marred by political infighting and betrayal. He clashed with political rivals and faced opposition from neighboring countries, leading to his eventual exile from Uruguay in 1820.

Artigas spent his final years in exile in Paraguay, where he continued to advocate for his vision of a free and united South America. He died in poverty and obscurity in 1850, but his legacy lived on, inspiring future generations of Uruguayans to uphold the values of independence, democracy, and social justice.

Today, Artigas is celebrated as a national hero in Uruguay, with monuments, memorials, and public holidays dedicated to his memory. His legacy continues to shape Uruguayan identity and politics, serving as a reminder of the country's resilient spirit and its ongoing quest for freedom and equality.

Rural Life: Insights into Uruguay's Agrarian Communities

Rural life in Uruguay offers a glimpse into the country's agrarian communities, where tradition, hard work, and a strong connection to the land shape daily life. Uruguay's rural areas are primarily characterized by vast expanses of fertile farmland, rolling hills, and small agricultural communities scattered throughout the countryside.

Agriculture is the backbone of Uruguay's economy, with the country known for its production of beef, wool, dairy products, and grains. Rural communities play a vital role in sustaining these agricultural industries, with many families owning and operating small farms and ranches passed down through generations.

Livestock farming, particularly cattle ranching, is a cornerstone of rural life in Uruguay. The country boasts one of the highest ratios of cattle to people in the world, with millions of cattle grazing on the expansive grasslands known as the pampas. Ranchers raise cattle for meat production, with beef exports contributing significantly to Uruguay's economy.

In addition to cattle ranching, rural communities in Uruguay engage in sheep farming for wool production, dairy farming for milk and cheese, and crop cultivation, including soybeans, wheat, and rice. Many farmers practice sustainable and organic farming methods, prioritizing environmental conservation and animal welfare.

Life in Uruguay's agrarian communities is characterized by a close-knit sense of community and a strong connection to the land. Family and social gatherings are central to rural life, with events such as barbecues (asados), rodeos (jineteadas), and traditional festivals (fiestas patronales) providing opportunities for neighbors to come together and celebrate their shared heritage.

Education and healthcare services in rural areas are often provided through small schools and clinics, serving the needs of local residents. While some rural communities face challenges such as limited access to resources and infrastructure, many residents value the tranquility and natural beauty of rural life, choosing to live close to nature and away from the hustle and bustle of urban centers.

Overall, rural life in Uruguay offers a glimpse into a way of life that is deeply rooted in tradition, resilience, and the rhythms of nature. As the country continues to evolve, rural communities remain an integral part of Uruguay's cultural and economic landscape, preserving age-old traditions while embracing new opportunities for growth and development.

Urbanization and Modernization: Evolution of Uruguayan Cities

Urbanization and modernization have been transformative forces in shaping the landscape of Uruguayan cities, reflecting the country's socioeconomic development and evolving cultural identity. Uruguay's urbanization process began in the late 19th century with the rise of industrialization and the influx of European immigrants seeking opportunities in the New World. Montevideo, the capital city, emerged as the focal point of this urban growth, experiencing rapid expansion and modernization during the early 20th century.

As Uruguay's largest city and primary economic hub, Montevideo became a melting pot of cultures, attracting immigrants from Italy, Spain, Germany, and beyond. The city's diverse population contributed to its cosmopolitan atmosphere and laid the groundwork for its reputation as a cultural and commercial center.

Throughout the 20th century, Montevideo continued to grow and develop, with urbanization spreading outward from the city center to surrounding neighborhoods and suburbs. Modern infrastructure projects, including the construction of highways, bridges, and public transportation systems, facilitated this expansion and connected urban areas with rural communities.

Today, Montevideo is a bustling metropolis with a mix of architectural styles, ranging from colonial-era buildings in the historic Ciudad Vieja district to modern skyscrapers in the downtown business district. The city is known for its vibrant cultural scene, with theaters, museums, galleries, and music venues showcasing Uruguayan and international talent.

In addition to Montevideo, other Uruguayan cities have also experienced significant urbanization and modernization in recent decades. Cities such as Salto, Paysandú, and Rivera have grown in size and importance, fueled by economic development, infrastructure investments, and urban planning initiatives.

Urbanization has brought both opportunities and challenges to Uruguayan cities. On one hand, urban areas offer access to education, healthcare, employment, and cultural amenities, attracting residents from rural areas in search of a better quality of life. On the other hand, rapid urban growth has strained infrastructure, led to environmental degradation, and exacerbated social inequalities.

Despite these challenges, Uruguayan cities continue to evolve and adapt to the changing needs of their residents. Urban planning initiatives aimed at promoting sustainable development, improving public transportation, and revitalizing urban spaces have been implemented to address the complex issues facing modern cities.

Overall, the evolution of Uruguayan cities reflects the country's ongoing transition from a predominantly rural society to an increasingly urbanized and modernized nation. As cities continue to grow and change, they will play a critical role in shaping Uruguay's future trajectory and defining its identity on the global stage.

Uruguay's Educational System: Commitment to Learning and Growth

Uruguay's educational system reflects the country's commitment to providing accessible and quality education to all its citizens. Education is considered a fundamental right enshrined in the Uruguayan Constitution, with the government playing a central role in ensuring equitable access to educational opportunities from early childhood through higher education.

The education system in Uruguay is divided into several levels, including preschool, primary education, secondary education, and higher education. Preschool education is available to children aged three to five and is not mandatory, but widely attended as it is part of the National Early Childhood Education Plan.

Primary education in Uruguay is compulsory and free for children aged six to eleven, encompassing six years of schooling. The curriculum focuses on developing foundational skills in literacy, numeracy, and social studies, with an emphasis on fostering critical thinking, creativity, and citizenship.

Secondary education in Uruguay consists of three years of schooling, typically attended by students aged twelve to fifteen. Secondary schools offer a general education curriculum that prepares students for further academic study or entry into the workforce. In addition to core subjects such as language, mathematics, and science, students have the opportunity to choose elective courses in areas of interest.

Uruguay places a strong emphasis on inclusive education, striving to ensure that students with disabilities, learning difficulties, or special needs receive appropriate support and accommodations to fully participate in the educational process. Special education services are available in both mainstream and specialized schools, with a focus on individualized instruction and support.

In recent years, Uruguay has implemented several educational reforms aimed at improving the quality and equity of its education system. One of the most significant reforms is the "Plan Ceibal," which aims to provide all students and teachers with access to digital technology and internet connectivity. Through initiatives like the "One Laptop per Child" program, Uruguay has distributed laptops and tablets to students and teachers nationwide, transforming teaching and learning in the digital age.

Higher education in Uruguay is provided by universities and technical institutes, offering a wide range of undergraduate and graduate programs in various fields of study. The National University of Uruguay (UdelaR) is the country's largest and most prestigious university, offering programs in humanities, sciences, engineering, medicine, and more.

Overall, Uruguay's educational system reflects a commitment to promoting lifelong learning, fostering social inclusion, and preparing citizens to contribute to society and the global community. Through continuous investment in education and innovative reforms, Uruguay aims to ensure that all its citizens have the knowledge, skills, and opportunities to succeed in the 21st century.

Healthcare in Uruguay: Accessible and Quality Services

Healthcare in Uruguay is characterized by its commitment to providing accessible and quality services to all its citizens. The country boasts a universal healthcare system that ensures comprehensive coverage for medical care, medications, and treatments, regardless of income or employment status. This system, known as the National Integrated Health System (SNIS), guarantees access to healthcare as a fundamental right enshrined in the Uruguayan Constitution.

Under the SNIS, healthcare services are provided through a network of public and private providers, including hospitals, clinics, and health centers, distributed across the country. The public healthcare sector is funded primarily through taxes and government contributions, while the private sector operates alongside it, offering additional services to those who can afford them.

One of the hallmarks of Uruguay's healthcare system is its emphasis on preventive care and primary healthcare services. Health promotion and disease prevention programs are implemented nationwide, focusing on issues such as vaccination, maternal and child health, chronic disease management, and healthy lifestyle promotion. Primary healthcare teams, comprising doctors, nurses, and other healthcare professionals, play a key role in delivering preventive care and addressing the healthcare needs of local communities.

In addition to primary care, Uruguay's healthcare system provides comprehensive coverage for a wide range of medical services, including specialist consultations, diagnostic tests, surgeries, and emergency care. Patients have the freedom to choose their healthcare providers, whether they prefer public or private facilities, and access to specialized care is available through referral from primary care physicians.

Pharmaceutical services are also an integral part of Uruguay's healthcare system, with a national drug formulary ensuring access to essential medications at affordable prices. Medications are dispensed through a network of pharmacies, both public and private, with subsidies available for those who qualify for assistance.

Uruguay's healthcare system is supported by a robust regulatory framework and oversight mechanisms to ensure quality and safety standards are met. Healthcare professionals are required to adhere to strict licensing and accreditation requirements, and healthcare facilities undergo regular inspections to maintain compliance with regulatory standards.

Overall, Uruguay's healthcare system is widely regarded as one of the best in Latin America, with indicators such as life expectancy, infant mortality, and access to healthcare services consistently ranking among the highest in the region. Despite facing challenges such as resource constraints and increasing demand for services, Uruguay remains committed to providing accessible, equitable, and quality healthcare to its population.

Environmental Conservation Efforts: Protecting Uruguay's Natural Treasures

Environmental conservation efforts in Uruguay are vital to safeguarding the country's natural treasures and preserving its biodiversity for future generations. Uruguay is home to diverse ecosystems, including coastal habitats, grasslands, wetlands, and forests, each playing a critical role in supporting a wide range of plant and animal species.

One of Uruguay's most significant environmental conservation efforts is focused on protecting its coastal areas, including beaches, dunes, and estuaries. These coastal habitats are essential breeding grounds for marine life, including seabirds, sea turtles, and seals, and provide important ecosystem services such as erosion control and carbon sequestration.

In recent years, Uruguay has implemented various measures to conserve its coastal ecosystems, including the establishment of protected areas and conservation zones, the enforcement of regulations to limit coastal development, and the promotion of sustainable tourism practices. These efforts aim to balance economic development with environmental protection, ensuring that coastal areas remain healthy and vibrant for future generations to enjoy.

In addition to coastal conservation, Uruguay is also focused on preserving its grasslands, which cover a significant portion of the country's interior. Grasslands, known as the pampas, are home to diverse plant and animal species, including iconic wildlife such as the South American ostrich (ñandú) and the capybara. Conservation efforts in the pampas include the creation of national parks and nature reserves, as well as initiatives to restore degraded grassland habitats and promote sustainable grazing practices.

Wetlands are another priority for environmental conservation in Uruguay, as these valuable ecosystems provide critical habitat for migratory birds, fish, and other wildlife. Uruguay is a signatory to the Ramsar Convention on Wetlands, an international treaty aimed at conserving and sustainably managing wetland areas. The country has designated several wetlands of international importance, such as the Bañados del Este Biosphere Reserve, for protection and conservation.

Forests are also a key focus of environmental conservation efforts in Uruguay, with the country's native forests facing threats from deforestation, agricultural expansion, and illegal logging. Uruguay has implemented reforestation programs and forest management initiatives to restore degraded forest ecosystems and protect remaining areas of native vegetation. The country is also working to promote sustainable forestry practices and certification schemes to ensure that timber harvesting is carried out responsibly and sustainably.

Overall, Uruguay's environmental conservation efforts are guided by a commitment to sustainable development, biodiversity conservation, and climate resilience. By protecting its natural treasures and embracing conservation practices, Uruguay aims to safeguard its environment for future generations and promote the well-being of its people and wildlife alike.

Uruguay's Wine Industry: From Vineyard to Glass

Uruguay's wine industry is a fascinating journey from vineyard to glass, showcasing the country's rich viticultural heritage and commitment to producing high-quality wines. While Uruguay may not be as well-known for its wines as some of its South American neighbors, such as Argentina and Chile, it boasts a long history of winemaking dating back to the colonial era.

The wine industry in Uruguay is primarily concentrated in the southern region of the country, where favorable climatic conditions and diverse terroirs provide ideal growing conditions for grape cultivation. The most commonly grown grape varieties in Uruguay include Tannat, a red grape indigenous to the region, as well as Merlot, Cabernet Sauvignon, and Chardonnay.

Tannat is considered Uruguay's flagship grape variety, known for producing bold, full-bodied red wines with rich flavors of dark fruit, spice, and earthy undertones. The grape thrives in Uruguay's temperate climate and well-drained soils, particularly in the regions of Canelones and Salto.

Uruguay's wine industry is characterized by its focus on small-scale, boutique wineries, many of which are family-owned and operated. These wineries prioritize quality over quantity, employing traditional winemaking techniques and handcrafting wines that reflect the unique characteristics of the terroir.

In recent years, Uruguay's wine industry has garnered international recognition for its high-quality wines, earning accolades and awards at prestigious wine competitions around the world. The country's Tannat wines, in particular, have gained a loyal following among wine enthusiasts for their distinctive flavors and age-worthiness.

Uruguayan winemakers are also experimenting with new grape varieties and winemaking styles, diversifying their offerings to appeal to a broader audience. In addition to Tannat, wineries produce a wide range of varietal wines, blends, sparkling wines, and dessert wines, showcasing the country's winemaking prowess and innovation.

Visitors to Uruguay have the opportunity to explore its wine regions through guided tours and tastings at local wineries, where they can learn about the winemaking process, sample different wines, and experience the beauty of the vineyards firsthand. Wine tourism has become increasingly popular in Uruguay, attracting visitors from around the world to discover the country's hidden gem of a wine industry.

Overall, Uruguay's wine industry is a testament to the passion and dedication of its winemakers, who continue to push the boundaries of quality and excellence in pursuit of crafting world-class wines. Whether you're a seasoned oenophile or a curious wine enthusiast, Uruguay's wine country offers a truly unforgettable experience for all who venture to explore it.

Banking and Finance: Navigating Uruguay's Financial Sector

Uruguay's banking and finance sector is a key pillar of its economy, providing essential services to individuals, businesses, and investors both domestically and internationally. The country's financial system is characterized by stability, transparency, and a strong regulatory framework that promotes confidence and trust among stakeholders.

The Central Bank of Uruguay serves as the primary regulatory authority overseeing the country's banking and financial sector, responsible for supervising banks, financial institutions, and capital markets to ensure compliance with regulations and safeguard the stability of the financial system.

Uruguay's banking sector is dominated by both domestic and foreign banks, offering a wide range of banking services including savings accounts, checking accounts, loans, mortgages, and investment products. Many of the country's largest banks are subsidiaries of international banking groups, providing access to global financial networks and expertise.

In addition to traditional banking services, Uruguay has developed a sophisticated financial infrastructure that includes capital markets, insurance companies, pension funds, and asset management firms. The country's capital markets offer opportunities for investors to buy and sell securities, including stocks, bonds, and derivatives, through regulated exchanges such as the Montevideo Stock Exchange.

Uruguay's financial sector has undergone significant modernization and digital transformation in recent years, with the adoption of electronic banking, mobile payment systems, and online trading platforms. These advancements have enhanced accessibility, efficiency, and convenience for customers, facilitating financial transactions and investment activities.

The country's regulatory environment emphasizes prudential supervision, risk management, and anti-money laundering measures to mitigate financial risks and maintain the integrity of the banking system. Uruguay has also implemented international standards and best practices in banking regulation and supervision, aligning its financial sector with global norms and requirements.

Uruguay's reputation as a safe and reliable financial jurisdiction has attracted foreign investors and offshore banking clients seeking stability, confidentiality, and legal certainty. The country's banking secrecy laws, while subject to international scrutiny and compliance with international tax regulations, provide privacy protection for account holders and investors.

Overall, Uruguay's banking and finance sector play a critical role in supporting economic growth, facilitating trade and investment, and providing financial services that meet the needs of a diverse clientele. With a commitment to transparency, stability, and innovation, Uruguay's financial sector continues to evolve and adapt to the changing dynamics of the global economy.

Festivals and Events: Celebrating Life in Uruguay

Festivals and events in Uruguay are vibrant celebrations that showcase the country's rich cultural heritage, diverse traditions, and zest for life. Throughout the year, Uruguayans come together to commemorate a variety of religious, historical, and cultural occasions, creating an atmosphere of joy, camaraderie, and festivity.

One of Uruguay's most renowned festivals is Carnival, a colorful and exuberant celebration that takes place in February or March, depending on the lunar calendar. Carnival in Uruguay is a time of music, dance, and revelry, with elaborate parades, street parties, and masked performers known as "murgas" and "candombes" taking center stage in cities and towns across the country. Carnival is deeply rooted in Afro-Uruguayan culture and traditions, incorporating elements of music, dance, and folklore that reflect the country's multicultural heritage.

Another highlight of Uruguay's festival calendar is Semana Criolla, or Creole Week, held annually in April at the Rural del Prado exhibition grounds in Montevideo. Semana Criolla is a celebration of gaucho culture and rural traditions, featuring equestrian events, folk music and dance performances, traditional food and crafts, and the crowning of the "paisano" and "paisana" (gaucho and gaucho girl) of the year. The festival provides a glimpse into Uruguay's cowboy heritage and the customs of its rural communities.

Religious festivals also play a significant role in Uruguay's cultural landscape, reflecting the country's Catholic heritage and the influence of European immigrants. Easter, Christmas, and other Christian holidays are celebrated with religious ceremonies, processions, and traditional rituals in churches and communities throughout Uruguay. In addition, patron saint festivals, such as the Feast of Saint Francis of Assisi in Canelones and the Feast of Our Lady of Lourdes in Paysandú, are observed with devotion and reverence by local communities.

Uruguayans also take pride in their national holidays, such as Independence Day on August 25th and Día de la Constitución (Constitution Day) on July 18th, which commemorate key moments in the country's history and the struggle for independence and democracy. These holidays are marked by patriotic ceremonies, flag-raising ceremonies, cultural events, and public gatherings, uniting Uruguayans in a spirit of national pride and solidarity.

In addition to traditional festivals, Uruguay hosts a variety of cultural events, music festivals, and international competitions that attract visitors from around the world. The Montevideo Jazz Festival, Punta del Este International Film Festival, and Uruguay Open tennis tournament are just a few examples of the diverse range of events that contribute to Uruguay's vibrant cultural scene and enrich the lives of its residents and visitors alike.

Indigenous Peoples of Uruguay: Preserving Cultural Heritage

The indigenous peoples of Uruguay have a rich and diverse cultural heritage that spans thousands of years, dating back to pre-Columbian times. Before the arrival of European colonizers, the territory that is now Uruguay was inhabited by several indigenous groups, including the Charrúa, Guaraní, and Chaná peoples, among others.

The Charrúa were one of the most prominent indigenous groups in Uruguay, known for their nomadic lifestyle, warrior culture, and resistance against Spanish colonization. They inhabited the region along the Uruguay River and the Atlantic coast, relying on hunting, fishing, and gathering for their sustenance. The Charrúa people were skilled horsemen and fierce defenders of their territory, resisting European incursions for centuries before ultimately being decimated by disease, warfare, and forced assimilation.

Despite the devastating impact of colonization, Uruguay's indigenous heritage perseveres through the efforts of modern-day indigenous communities and organizations. Today, Uruguay recognizes the contributions and rights of indigenous peoples through legislative measures, cultural initiatives, and social programs aimed at preserving and promoting their cultural heritage, language, and traditions.

The Constitution of Uruguay recognizes the rights of indigenous peoples and guarantees their participation in the country's political, economic, and social life. The government has established institutions such as the National Institute of Indigenous Affairs (INA) to support indigenous communities and promote their rights, including land tenure, education, healthcare, and cultural preservation.

Efforts to preserve indigenous culture and heritage in Uruguay include initiatives to document and revive traditional languages, such as Charrúa and Guaraní, through language revitalization programs and bilingual education initiatives. Cultural festivals, workshops, and community events provide opportunities for indigenous peoples to showcase their traditional crafts, music, dance, and oral traditions, fostering pride and cultural identity.

Land rights remain a key issue for indigenous communities in Uruguay, as many struggle to regain control over ancestral territories and protect sacred sites from encroachment and exploitation. Indigenous land claims are subject to legal recognition and restitution processes, but progress has been slow, with challenges related to land tenure, property rights, and competing interests from agricultural, mining, and development projects.

Despite these challenges, indigenous peoples in Uruguay continue to assert their rights, assert their cultural identity, and contribute to the country's multicultural heritage. Their resilience, creativity, and determination to preserve their cultural heritage serve as a testament to the enduring legacy of Uruguay's indigenous peoples and their ongoing struggle for recognition, justice, and equality.

Afro-Uruguayan   Culture:
Contributions and Influence

Afro-Uruguayan culture has left an indelible mark on the cultural landscape of Uruguay, enriching the country's music, dance, cuisine, language, and traditions with its vibrant and distinct contributions. The roots of Afro-Uruguayan culture can be traced back to the transatlantic slave trade, which brought enslaved Africans to Uruguay during the colonial period to work on plantations, ranches, and in households.

Despite the harsh conditions of slavery, Afro-Uruguayan communities managed to preserve their cultural heritage through music, dance, oral traditions, and spiritual practices. One of the most significant aspects of Afro-Uruguayan culture is its music, particularly the rhythmical beats of candombe. Candombe originated in the neighborhoods of Montevideo, where enslaved Africans would gather to play drums, dance, and celebrate their cultural identity. Today, candombe is an integral part of Uruguay's cultural identity, recognized as a UNESCO Intangible Cultural Heritage of Humanity.

The Afro-Uruguayan community has also made significant contributions to Uruguay's cuisine, introducing flavors and ingredients from African culinary traditions into the country's gastronomy. Dishes such as carapulcra (a stew made with dried beef and potatoes), mondongo (tripe soup), and feijoada (a Brazilian-inspired bean stew) reflect the influence of Afro-Uruguayan culinary heritage on the country's culinary repertoire.

In addition to music and cuisine, Afro-Uruguayan culture has influenced other aspects of Uruguayan society, including language, religion, and social customs. African words and expressions have been incorporated into Uruguayan Spanish, enriching the local lexicon and adding depth to the country's linguistic diversity.

Afro-Uruguayan religious practices, such as Candomblé and Umbanda, blend African spiritual beliefs with Catholicism and indigenous traditions, creating syncretic forms of worship that are deeply rooted in the Afro-Uruguayan community. These religious practices are celebrated through rituals, ceremonies, and festivals that honor African deities and ancestral spirits.

Despite facing historical discrimination and marginalization, Afro-Uruguayan communities have persevered and thrived, contributing to Uruguay's cultural mosaic and shaping its national identity. In recent years, there has been a growing recognition of Afro-Uruguayan culture and heritage, with efforts to promote cultural awareness, education, and social inclusion.

Today, Afro-Uruguayan cultural expressions are celebrated and embraced as integral parts of Uruguay's multicultural heritage, highlighting the resilience, creativity, and contributions of Afro-Uruguayan communities to the country's cultural richness and diversity.

Women's Rights and Gender Equality in Uruguay

In Uruguay, women's rights and gender equality have been significant areas of focus and progress over the past century. The country has made considerable strides in promoting women's empowerment, advancing gender equality, and combating discrimination and violence against women.

Uruguay was one of the first countries in Latin America to grant women the right to vote in 1932, setting a precedent for women's political participation and representation in the region. Since then, women in Uruguay have played increasingly prominent roles in politics, government, academia, business, and civil society, contributing to shaping the country's social and economic development.

In recent decades, Uruguay has implemented legislative reforms and policies aimed at promoting gender equality and protecting women's rights. The country has ratified international conventions and agreements related to women's rights, including the Convention on the Elimination of All Forms of Discrimination Against Women (CEDAW) and the Beijing Platform for Action.

Uruguay has also enacted laws to address gender-based violence and discrimination, including the Law on Comprehensive Protection of Women Against Gender-Based Violence, which provides legal mechanisms for preventing, punishing, and eradicating violence against women. The law established specialized courts, shelters, and support services for survivors of gender-based violence, as well as educational programs to raise awareness and promote gender equality.

The government of Uruguay has implemented affirmative action measures to promote gender parity and representation in decision-making positions, including quotas for women's participation in political parties, electoral lists, and public sector appointments. As a result, women's representation in parliament and local government has increased steadily, although challenges remain in achieving full gender equality in leadership roles.

Uruguay has also made significant progress in advancing women's reproductive rights and health, including access to contraception, prenatal care, and safe abortion services. The country legalized abortion in 2012, allowing women to access abortion services under certain conditions, such as risk to maternal health, fetal anomalies, or rape, marking a significant milestone in women's reproductive rights in Uruguay.

Despite these achievements, challenges persist in achieving full gender equality in Uruguay, particularly in addressing persistent gender gaps in employment, wages, education, and access to economic opportunities. Women continue to face barriers to full participation in the labor market, including occupational segregation, unequal pay, and limited access to leadership positions.

Uruguay recognizes the importance of gender mainstreaming and intersectionality in its policies and programs, acknowledging that gender equality is interconnected with other dimensions of social inequality, such as race, ethnicity, class, and sexual orientation. Efforts to promote gender equality in Uruguay are therefore holistic and inclusive, addressing multiple forms of discrimination and inequality.

Overall, Uruguay's commitment to women's rights and gender equality is evident in its legal framework, institutional mechanisms, and public policies aimed at advancing women's empowerment, combating gender-based violence, and promoting equal opportunities for all. While progress has been made, there is still work to be done to achieve full gender equality and social justice in Uruguay.

LGBTQ+ Rights and Acceptance in Uruguayan Society

In Uruguay, LGBTQ+ rights and acceptance have seen significant progress in recent years, positioning the country as a leader in LGBTQ+ rights within Latin America and the world. Uruguay has implemented legislative reforms and social initiatives aimed at promoting equality, combating discrimination, and protecting the rights of LGBTQ+ individuals.

One of the most notable milestones in Uruguay's LGBTQ+ rights journey was the legalization of same-sex marriage in 2013, making Uruguay the second country in Latin America and the twelfth in the world to recognize marriage equality. This landmark legislation represented a significant step forward in affirming the rights of LGBTQ+ couples to legally marry and enjoy the same rights and protections as heterosexual couples.

In addition to marriage equality, Uruguay has enacted comprehensive anti-discrimination laws that prohibit discrimination on the basis of sexual orientation and gender identity in employment, education, healthcare, housing, and other areas of public life. These laws aim to ensure equal treatment and opportunities for LGBTQ+ individuals and protect them from harassment, violence, and prejudice.

Uruguay has also implemented gender identity laws that recognize and affirm the rights of transgender and non-binary individuals to self-identify their gender and access legal recognition of their gender identity. The Gender Identity Law, passed in 2018, allows individuals to change their name and gender marker on official documents without undergoing medical or psychological interventions, simplifying the process of legal gender recognition and affirming the dignity and autonomy of transgender people.

The Uruguayan government has established institutional mechanisms and support services to promote LGBTQ+ rights and provide assistance to LGBTQ+ individuals facing discrimination or violence. The National Institute of Human Rights and Ombudsman's Office oversees human rights protection and advocacy, including LGBTQ+ rights, while civil society organizations such as Ovejas Negras and Colectivo OTRANS work to advance LGBTQ+ equality and visibility through education, advocacy, and community outreach.

Uruguay's progressive stance on LGBTQ+ rights is reflected in its broader cultural attitudes and societal acceptance of diverse sexual orientations and gender identities. LGBTQ+ individuals in Uruguay enjoy relatively high levels of social acceptance and support, with LGBTQ+ pride events, festivals, and marches celebrated openly and enthusiastically across the country.

While progress has been made in advancing LGBTQ+ rights and acceptance in Uruguay, challenges remain, including addressing stigma, discrimination, and violence against LGBTQ+ individuals, particularly transgender and gender-nonconforming people. There is ongoing advocacy and activism to promote LGBTQ+ rights and address systemic barriers to equality, including access to healthcare, education, employment, and legal recognition.

Overall, Uruguay's commitment to LGBTQ+ rights and acceptance reflects its values of inclusivity, diversity, and social justice, positioning the country as a beacon of progress and tolerance in the region. Through continued advocacy, education, and solidarity, Uruguay aims to build a society where all individuals, regardless of sexual orientation or gender identity, can live freely and authentically.

Architecture and Urban Design: Montevideo's Unique Aesthetics

Montevideo, the capital city of Uruguay, boasts a rich architectural heritage that reflects its diverse history, cultural influences, and urban development over the centuries. From colonial-era landmarks to modernist skyscrapers, Montevideo's architecture showcases a blend of styles, materials, and aesthetics that contribute to the city's unique character and charm.

One of the defining features of Montevideo's architecture is its eclectic mix of architectural styles, which reflect the city's history of colonization, immigration, and cultural exchange. The historic Ciudad Vieja (Old Town) is home to colonial-era buildings with Spanish, Portuguese, and Moorish influences, characterized by their ornate facades, wrought iron balconies, and cobblestone streets. These architectural gems provide a glimpse into Montevideo's colonial past and serve as a testament to the city's rich heritage.

As Montevideo grew and modernized in the late 19th and early 20th centuries, new architectural styles emerged, influenced by European trends and urban planning principles. The city's downtown area features elegant art deco and neoclassical buildings, many of which were constructed during Uruguay's economic boom in the early 20th century. These architectural gems, adorned with intricate detailing and grand facades, reflect Montevideo's prosperity and ambition during this period.

In the mid-20th century, Montevideo experienced a period of rapid urbanization and expansion, leading to the construction of modernist buildings and infrastructure projects that transformed the city's skyline. Architects such as Julio Vilamajó and Carlos Ott left their mark on Montevideo with iconic buildings like the Palacio Legislativo (Legislative Palace) and the Torre de las Telecomunicaciones (Telecommunications Tower), which showcase innovative design and engineering.

Montevideo's architectural landscape continues to evolve, with contemporary architects and designers embracing sustainable practices, innovative technologies, and creative solutions to address the city's urban challenges. The revitalization of historic neighborhoods, such as Ciudad Vieja and Barrio Sur, has led to the adaptive reuse of old buildings and the integration of modern amenities, creating vibrant and livable spaces for residents and visitors alike.

In recent years, Montevideo has also seen the emergence of cutting-edge architectural projects and cultural institutions that contribute to the city's cultural vibrancy and global appeal. The new Antel Arena, designed by renowned architect Rafael Viñoly, serves as a multipurpose venue for concerts, sporting events, and conferences, while the Museo Nacional de Artes Visuales (National Museum of

Visual Arts) showcases Uruguay's rich artistic heritage in a contemporary setting.

Montevideo's architectural diversity and innovation reflect the city's dynamic spirit and commitment to preserving its heritage while embracing the opportunities of the future. Whether wandering through its historic streets or marveling at its modern landmarks, visitors to Montevideo are treated to a visual feast of architectural delights that capture the essence of Uruguay's capital city.

Traditional Crafts and Artisans: Preserving Cultural Traditions

In Uruguay, traditional crafts and artisans play a vital role in preserving the country's rich cultural heritage and passing down centuries-old techniques and traditions from generation to generation. From intricate leatherwork to colorful textiles and ceramics, Uruguay's traditional crafts reflect the country's diverse cultural influences and artistic creativity.

One of the most renowned traditional crafts in Uruguay is mate gourd carving. The mate gourd, used to prepare and drink mate, a traditional herbal tea, is intricately carved with elaborate designs depicting scenes from nature, folklore, and everyday life. Artisans meticulously hand-carve each gourd using specialized tools, creating unique and highly detailed works of art that are cherished by locals and collectors alike.

Leatherworking is another traditional craft that has deep roots in Uruguayan culture. The country's vast ranching heritage and abundance of high-quality leather have inspired generations of artisans to create finely crafted leather goods, including saddles, belts, shoes, and accessories. Uruguayan leatherworkers are known for their skillful craftsmanship and attention to detail, producing durable and stylish products that showcase the natural beauty of leather.

Textile weaving is also an integral part of Uruguay's traditional crafts, with artisans using techniques such as handloom weaving and knitting to create a wide range of textiles, including blankets, rugs, and garments. Many of these textiles feature intricate patterns and vibrant colors, reflecting the country's indigenous, African, and European influences. Uruguayan textiles are prized for their quality, craftsmanship, and unique aesthetic appeal.

Ceramics are another traditional craft that thrives in Uruguay, with artisans producing pottery, tiles, and sculptures using techniques that date back centuries. The country's rich clay deposits and skilled artisans have led to the creation of diverse ceramic styles, ranging from rustic earthenware to intricately glazed ceramics. Uruguayan ceramics are often inspired by the natural beauty of the country's landscapes, flora, and fauna, as well as its cultural heritage and traditions.

Woodworking is also a cherished traditional craft in Uruguay, with artisans creating beautiful handcrafted furniture, carvings, and musical instruments using locally sourced woods such as cedar, walnut, and jacaranda. Uruguayan woodworkers are admired for their mastery of traditional techniques and their ability to transform raw materials into exquisite works of art that showcase the natural beauty and versatility of wood.

Throughout Uruguay, traditional crafts and artisans are celebrated and supported through cultural festivals, artisan markets, and educational programs that promote the preservation and appreciation of these time-honored traditions. By preserving and promoting traditional crafts, Uruguay honors its cultural heritage, fosters creativity and innovation, and sustains livelihoods for artisans and their communities for generations to come.

Transportation and Infrastructure: Getting Around Uruguay

In Uruguay, transportation and infrastructure play a crucial role in facilitating the movement of people and goods across the country's diverse landscapes and urban centers. With a well-developed transportation network and modern infrastructure, Uruguay offers various options for getting around efficiently and comfortably.

One of the primary modes of transportation in Uruguay is the road network, which consists of well-maintained highways, paved roads, and rural routes that connect cities, towns, and rural areas across the country. The road network provides convenient access to Uruguay's diverse regions, including its coastal resorts, agricultural heartland, and historic towns. Travelers can navigate Uruguay's roads by car, bus, or motorcycle, enjoying scenic drives and exploring the country at their own pace.

Uruguay's public transportation system is efficient and reliable, with buses serving as the primary mode of urban and intercity travel. In Montevideo, the capital city, a network of bus routes connects neighborhoods, suburbs, and key attractions, providing affordable and accessible transportation for residents and visitors alike. Intercity buses offer comfortable and affordable travel between major cities and towns, with frequent departures and modern amenities onboard.

Rail transportation also plays a role in Uruguay's transportation system, although to a lesser extent than road and bus travel. The country's railway network primarily serves freight transport, moving agricultural products, minerals, and other goods between production centers and ports for export. However, efforts have been made to revitalize passenger rail services, with tourist trains operating on scenic routes such as the Tren del Vino (Wine Train) in the Canelones wine region.

Air travel is another important aspect of Uruguay's transportation infrastructure, with several airports serving domestic and international flights. The Carrasco International Airport, located near Montevideo, is the country's main gateway for international travel, offering direct flights to major cities in South America, North America, Europe, and beyond. Regional airports in cities like Punta del Este, Colonia del Sacramento, and Salto provide domestic flights to various destinations within Uruguay.

Uruguay's maritime infrastructure supports trade and transportation along its extensive coastline, with ports and harbors handling cargo shipments, cruise ships, and ferry services. The Port of Montevideo is the country's largest and busiest port, serving as a vital hub for maritime trade and commerce in the region. Ferries operate between Montevideo and destinations such as Buenos Aires, Argentina, and Colonia del Sacramento, providing convenient and scenic transportation across the Río de la Plata.

In addition to traditional modes of transportation, Uruguay is embracing modern innovations such as ride-sharing services, cycling infrastructure, and electric mobility solutions to enhance mobility and reduce emissions. The country's commitment to sustainable transportation and infrastructure development reflects its vision for a more accessible, efficient, and environmentally friendly transportation system that meets the needs of its residents and visitors in the 21st century.

Learning Spanish: Essentials for Navigating Uruguayan Society

Learning Spanish is essential for navigating Uruguayan society and fully immersing oneself in the country's culture, communication, and daily life. Spanish, the official language of Uruguay, is spoken by nearly the entire population and serves as the primary means of communication in all aspects of society, including education, business, government, and social interactions.

For visitors and expatriates alike, having a basic understanding of Spanish is invaluable for getting around, interacting with locals, and accessing essential services. While English may be spoken in tourist areas and by some professionals, particularly in urban centers like Montevideo, knowing Spanish opens doors to deeper connections and cultural experiences.

Uruguay's Spanish, often referred to as Rioplatense Spanish, has its unique characteristics and dialectal features influenced by regional variations and historical factors. While similar to the Spanish spoken in neighboring Argentina, Uruguayan Spanish has its distinct pronunciation, vocabulary, and idiomatic expressions that reflect the country's cultural identity and linguistic heritage.

To learn Spanish effectively in Uruguay, individuals have various options, including language schools, private tutors, online courses, and immersion programs. Language schools and institutes offer structured Spanish courses tailored to different proficiency levels, from beginner to advanced, with classes covering grammar, vocabulary, pronunciation, and conversation practice.

Private tutors provide personalized instruction and flexibility for learners seeking individualized attention and focused learning goals. Online courses and language learning platforms offer convenience and accessibility, allowing learners to study Spanish at their own pace and schedule from anywhere in the world.

Immersion programs provide the most immersive language learning experience, allowing participants to live and study in Uruguay while fully immersed in the Spanish language and culture. By living with host families, attending classes, and engaging in daily activities and interactions in Spanish, participants can accelerate their language acquisition and deepen their cultural understanding.

Beyond formal instruction, practicing Spanish in real-life situations is essential for mastering the language and building fluency. Engaging with native speakers, whether through conversations, social events, or cultural activities, provides valuable opportunities to apply and reinforce language skills in authentic contexts.

In addition to spoken Spanish, understanding written Spanish is crucial for navigating everyday tasks such as reading signs, menus, transportation schedules, and official documents. Developing reading skills through exposure to newspapers, books, and online resources helps learners expand their vocabulary and comprehension abilities.

Overall, learning Spanish opens doors to richer cultural experiences, deeper connections with locals, and greater opportunities for exploration and engagement in Uruguay. Whether for short-term visits or long-term stays, investing in Spanish language skills enriches the travel experience and fosters meaningful connections with the people and culture of Uruguay.

Folklore and Superstitions: Insights into Uruguayan Beliefs

In Uruguay, folklore and superstitions hold a significant place in the cultural fabric of the country, offering insights into the beliefs, traditions, and values of its people. Rooted in a blend of indigenous, African, and European influences, Uruguayan folklore encompasses a diverse array of myths, legends, rituals, and customs that have been passed down through generations.

One prominent aspect of Uruguayan folklore is the belief in supernatural beings and mythical creatures that inhabit the country's landscapes. Among these are the "lobizones," or werewolves, which are said to roam the countryside under the light of the full moon, and the "yaguares," or jaguars, which are believed to possess shapeshifting abilities and magical powers.

Another popular figure in Uruguayan folklore is the "Luz Mala," or evil light, a mysterious phenomenon described as a glowing orb that appears in remote areas at night, leading travelers astray and causing misfortune to those who encounter it. Many believe that the Luz Mala is the restless spirit of someone who died tragically or unjustly and is destined to wander the earth in search of peace. Superstitions also play a significant role in Uruguayan culture, with many people adhering to traditional beliefs and practices to ward off bad luck and evil spirits. For example, it is common for people to avoid walking under ladders, crossing paths with black cats, or breaking mirrors, as these actions are believed to bring about misfortune.

Certain rituals and ceremonies are performed to protect against malevolent forces and ensure good fortune. For instance, some Uruguayan families hang garlic or red peppers near doorways to ward off evil spirits, while others light candles or burn incense during religious festivals and special occasions to invoke blessings and protection.

Uruguayan folklore is also rich in music, dance, and storytelling traditions that celebrate the country's cultural heritage and reflect the rhythms of everyday life. Traditional folk music genres such as "candombe," "milonga," and "murga" incorporate elements of African percussion, Spanish guitar, and indigenous melodies, providing a vibrant soundtrack to festivals, celebrations, and community gatherings.

Throughout Uruguay, folklore festivals and events bring together performers, artisans, and enthusiasts to celebrate the country's rich cultural heritage and showcase traditional music, dance, costumes, and rituals. These gatherings provide opportunities for people of all ages to connect with their roots, learn about their heritage, and keep traditions alive for future generations.

In conclusion, folklore and superstitions offer valuable insights into Uruguayan beliefs, values, and cultural identity, reflecting a deep connection to the land, the spirits of the ancestors, and the mysteries of the natural world. By embracing and preserving these traditions, Uruguayans honor their cultural heritage and keep alive the stories and customs that have shaped their collective identity for centuries.

Business Etiquette and Customs: Navigating Uruguayan Professional Environment

In Uruguay, understanding and adhering to business etiquette and customs are essential for navigating the professional environment and building successful relationships with colleagues, clients, and partners. While Uruguayan business culture shares similarities with other Latin American countries, it also has its unique customs and practices shaped by local traditions, values, and social norms.

One key aspect of Uruguayan business etiquette is the emphasis on personal relationships and mutual trust. Building rapport and establishing a sense of camaraderie with colleagues and business associates are crucial for fostering productive working relationships. In Uruguayan culture, it is common to engage in small talk and socialize with colleagues before discussing business matters, as relationships are valued as much as professional competence.

Formality and respect are important in Uruguayan business interactions, particularly when addressing senior colleagues or clients. It is customary to use titles and last names when addressing individuals in professional settings, followed by a handshake or a warm greeting. Demonstrating courtesy, politeness, and humility in communication helps to establish a positive impression and foster goodwill in business dealings.

Punctuality is another aspect of Uruguayan business culture that is highly valued. While meetings and appointments may start slightly later than scheduled, it is still important to arrive on time as a sign of respect for others' time and commitments. However, flexibility and understanding are also appreciated, as unforeseen delays or changes in plans can occur.

When it comes to business attire, Uruguayan professionals typically dress conservatively and formally, especially in corporate environments and during business meetings. Men often wear suits and ties, while women opt for professional attire such as dresses, skirts, or pantsuits. Dressing neatly and professionally conveys professionalism and respect for the business environment.

In terms of communication style, Uruguayan professionals tend to value clarity, directness, and honesty. It is important to express oneself clearly and concisely, avoiding ambiguity or vague language in business discussions. At the same time, maintaining a diplomatic and tactful approach is essential for preserving harmony and avoiding conflict in professional relationships.

Networking is a common practice in Uruguayan business culture, with professionals often attending industry events, conferences, and business gatherings to expand their contacts and build connections. Building a strong network of contacts can open doors to new opportunities and collaborations in the Uruguayan business community.

In conclusion, understanding and respecting business etiquette and customs are essential for navigating the professional environment in Uruguay. By adhering to cultural norms, building relationships, and demonstrating professionalism and respect, individuals can successfully integrate into the Uruguayan business culture and forge productive partnerships in the dynamic and vibrant business landscape of the country.

Future Perspectives: Challenges and Opportunities for Uruguay

Looking towards the future, Uruguay faces a mix of challenges and opportunities that will shape its trajectory in the years to come. One of the key challenges is ensuring sustainable economic growth while addressing income inequality and social disparities. Despite its reputation as one of the most economically developed countries in Latin America, Uruguay still grapples with income inequality, particularly between urban and rural areas and among different socioeconomic groups. Addressing these disparities will require targeted policies aimed at promoting inclusive growth, expanding access to education and healthcare, and creating opportunities for marginalized communities.

Another challenge is navigating the global economic landscape and external shocks, such as fluctuations in commodity prices and trade disruptions. As a small open economy, Uruguay is vulnerable to external factors beyond its control, making it crucial for policymakers to adopt prudent fiscal and monetary policies to safeguard against economic volatility and mitigate risks.

Furthermore, Uruguay faces environmental challenges, including climate change, deforestation, and pollution, which threaten its natural resources and biodiversity. Protecting the environment and promoting sustainable development are essential for preserving Uruguay's natural treasures for future generations. Embracing renewable energy sources, implementing conservation initiatives, and adopting eco-friendly practices across industries will be critical for mitigating environmental degradation and promoting long-term sustainability.

Despite these challenges, Uruguay also possesses significant opportunities for growth and development. The country's strategic location as a gateway to Mercosur, South America's leading trade bloc, presents opportunities for expanding trade and investment ties with neighboring countries and international partners. Strengthening regional integration and fostering economic cooperation can enhance Uruguay's competitiveness and unlock new markets for its goods and services.

Moreover, Uruguay's rich natural resources, including fertile agricultural land, abundant water resources, and renewable energy potential, position it as a promising hub for sustainable development and innovation. By leveraging its strengths in agriculture, agribusiness, technology, and renewable energy, Uruguay can capitalize on emerging opportunities in the global market and drive economic growth and diversification.

In addition, Uruguay boasts a well-educated workforce, a strong institutional framework, and a culture of innovation and entrepreneurship, providing a solid foundation for future prosperity. Investing in education, research, and innovation can further enhance Uruguay's human capital and foster creativity, productivity, and competitiveness in the global economy.

Furthermore, Uruguay's commitment to democracy, social cohesion, and human rights sets it apart as a stable and progressive nation in the region. By upholding democratic principles, promoting social inclusion, and respecting diversity, Uruguay can strengthen its social fabric and foster a more equitable and inclusive society for all its citizens.

Overall, navigating the future requires a proactive and multidimensional approach that addresses economic, social, environmental, and geopolitical challenges while seizing opportunities for growth, innovation, and sustainable development. By harnessing its strengths, embracing change, and fostering collaboration and dialogue, Uruguay can chart a course towards a brighter and more prosperous future for its people and the generations to come.

Epilogue

As we conclude our exploration of Uruguay, it's important to reflect on the journey we've taken through this diverse and captivating country. Throughout this book, we've delved into Uruguay's rich history, vibrant culture, stunning landscapes, and dynamic society, uncovering the many facets that make it a unique and fascinating destination.

From its indigenous heritage and colonial past to its struggles for independence and democratic evolution, Uruguay's history is a tapestry of resilience, perseverance, and transformation. We've traced the footsteps of its national hero, Jose Gervasio Artigas, and explored the legacy of his revolutionary spirit, which continues to inspire generations of Uruguayans today.

We've ventured into the bustling streets of Montevideo, the vibrant capital city, where modernity meets tradition in a blend of architectural marvels, cultural landmarks, and bustling markets. We've strolled along the cobblestone streets of Colonia del Sacramento, a UNESCO World Heritage site, and marveled at its well-preserved colonial architecture and scenic waterfront.

We've soaked in the sun-drenched beaches of Punta del Este, the playground of the rich and famous, and experienced the laid-back charm of coastal towns like Punta del Diablo and La Paloma. We've explored the rugged beauty of Uruguay's interior, from the rolling hills of the countryside to the expansive plains of the Pampas, where gaucho culture thrives.

We've savored the flavors of Uruguayan cuisine, from sizzling asados and hearty chivitos to delicate seafood dishes and indulgent dulce de leche desserts. We've raised a mate gourd with locals, sharing in the communal ritual of sipping Uruguay's beloved national beverage and connecting with the rhythms of daily life.

We've celebrated alongside Uruguayans during Carnival, a vibrant spectacle of music, dance, and color that fills the streets with energy and excitement. We've immersed ourselves in the sounds of tango and candombe, the soulful rhythms that echo through Uruguay's musical traditions and speak to its cultural heritage.

We've explored the diverse ecosystems of Uruguay, from the lush wetlands of the Esteros del Ibera to the rugged beauty of Cabo Polonio and the remote wilderness of Valle del Lunarejo. We've encountered a rich array of wildlife, from capybaras and caimans to sea lions and whales, highlighting Uruguay's commitment to environmental conservation and biodiversity protection.

As we bid farewell to Uruguay, let us carry with us the memories, experiences, and lessons learned from our journey through this enchanting land. May we continue to cherish and celebrate the beauty, diversity, and resilience of Uruguay and its people, and may our exploration inspire a deeper appreciation for the wonders of this remarkable country.

Made in the USA
Las Vegas, NV
17 November 2024